WITHDRAWN

RAIN FOREST

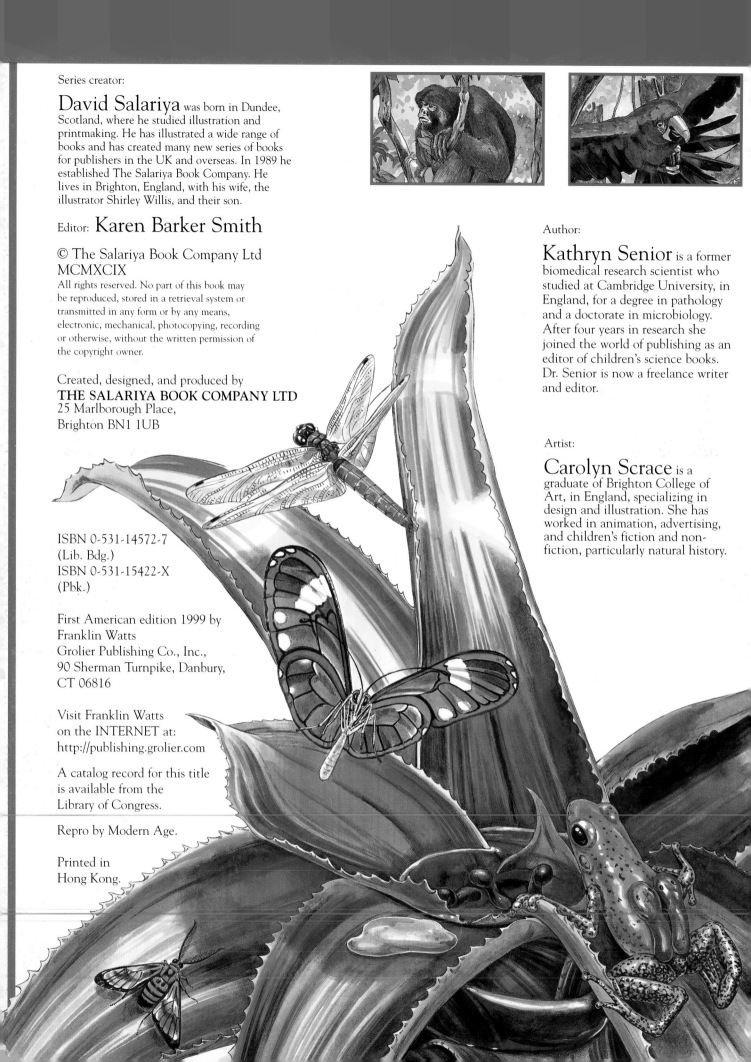

Series creator:

David Salariya was born in Dundee, Scotland, where he studied illustration and printmaking. He has illustrated a wide range of books and has created many new series of books for publishers in the UK and overseas. In 1989 he established The Salariya Book Company. He lives in Brighton, England, with his wife, the illustrator Shirley Willis, and their son.

Editor: **Karen Barker Smith**

Created, designed, and produced by
THE SALARIYA BOOK COMPANY LTD
25 Marlborough Place,
Brighton BN1 1UB

ISBN 0-531-14572-7
(Lib. Bdg.)
ISBN 0-531-15422-X
(Pbk.)

First American edition 1999 by
Franklin Watts
Grolier Publishing Co., Inc.,
90 Sherman Turnpike, Danbury,
CT 06816

Visit Franklin Watts
on the INTERNET at:
http://publishing.grolier.com

A catalog record for this title
is available from the
Library of Congress.

Repro by Modern Age.

Printed in
Hong Kong.

Author:

Kathryn Senior is a former biomedical research scientist who studied at Cambridge University, in England, for a degree in pathology and a doctorate in microbiology. After four years in research she joined the world of publishing as an editor of children's science books. Dr. Senior is now a freelance writer and editor.

Artist:

Carolyn Scrace is a graduate of Brighton College of Art, in England, specializing in design and illustration. She has worked in animation, advertising, and children's fiction and non-fiction, particularly natural history.

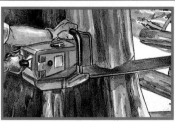

RAIN FOREST

Written by
KATHRYN SENIOR

Illustrated by
CAROLYN SCRACE

Created and designed by
DAVID SALARIYA

W
FRANKLIN WATTS
A Division of Grolier Publishing
NEW YORK • LONDON • HONG KONG • SYDNEY
DANBURY, CONNECTICUT

Contents

What Is a Rain Forest?

Rain forests are wet most of the time because of the 80 inches (200 centimeters) or more of rain that falls on them every year. They do exist in regions other than the tropics, but usually the term "rain forest" refers to those found on or near the equator.

There are several different types of rain forests. Lowland rain forests thrive at low altitudes and are the most extensive. The canopy is about 148 feet (45 meters) above the ground and forms a dense covering with few gaps between the trees. Some taller trees jut out to heights of over 197 feet (60 meters).

Several lowland rain forests are so close to rivers, they are permanently flooded. Mangrove rain forests are those that have formed in such flooded areas. The mangrove trees survive by growing roots that stick above the water.

Montane rain forests are found at higher altitudes, where it tends to be slightly colder. For this reason, the trees there do not grow as high – about 50–100 feet (15–30 meters) is the usual height of the canopy.

Extracts from more than 5,000 plant and animal species found in rain forests are used in food, medicine, and other products. At least 3,000 plant species that grow in the rain forests are known to contain compounds that can be used to develop new drugs to treat cancer. As the rain forests disappear, so do our chances of finding further useful substances in them.

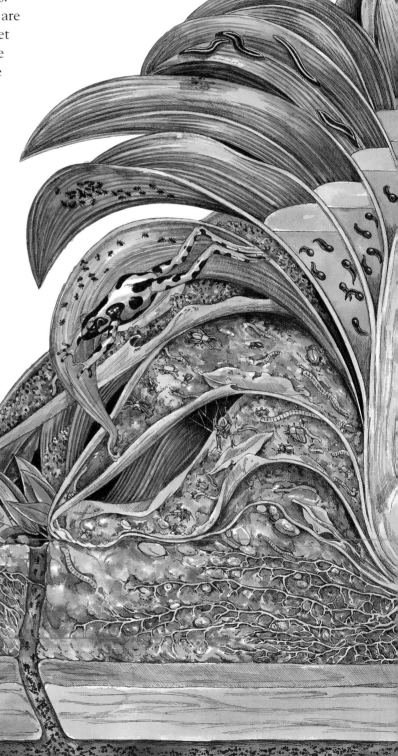

Before human beings existed, tropical rain forests of all types covered more than 8 million square miles (20.7 million square kilometers) of the planet. Forty million acres (16.2 million hectares) of rainforest are destroyed every year when trees are cut down for timber, paper pulp, and other wood products. By the end of the year 2000, there will be fewer than 3.4 million square miles (8.8 square kilometers) of rain forest left. The areas of rain forest that still exist today are shown on the maps below.

Less than 5 percent of the world's tropical rain forests are in protected national parks. The other 95 percent can be plundered for valuable natural resources. As long as the destruction continues, one rain forest species becomes extinct every 15 minutes. If our use of the earth's tropical rain forests does not change, they will all have disappeared by the year 2200. Approximately 25 percent of the planet's species will already be extinct by the middle of the 21st century.

Packed with Plants

The rain forest is a living, three-dimensional mosaic of plants. The canopy, the continuous cover provided by broad-leaved evergreen trees, towers as high as 197 feet (60 meters) above the ground. Under the thickest parts of the canopy, few other plants are able to grow. Where the top layer is less dense, a rich ground level of ferns, herbs, and mosses springs up. Different species and individual leaves jostle to catch the light as it filters through the plants above.

Climbing plants have their roots in the ground but use taller trees as support. Rattan palms have a barbed stem and use brute force to grow up and hook onto surrounding trees. They can reach a length of 197 feet (60 meters) or more, winding their way up and across different trees, until they are in a good position in the sun.

In Ghana, an area of rain forest covering 1.2 acres (0.5 hectares) (the size of a large garden) was shown to contain 350 different plant species.

One single tree in the rain forest of West Africa was found to support 47 different species of orchids.

In Costa Rica, the La Selva Forest Reserve contains as many plant species as all Britain, but in an area that is 17,000 times smaller.

Between 50 and 90 percent of the plant species that exist on earth are found in the rain forests, even though the rain forests cover just over 10 percent of the total land surface area.

Bromeliad

Pike-headed vine snake

Orchids produce some of the most beautiful flowers in the world. Their color and fragrance attract insects, which come and pollinate them. Only when pollen from another orchid has been placed in the female part of a flower is the orchid able to set seed and reproduce. Some orchids even copy the smell and shape of female insects so that male insects try to mate with the orchid. When they do this, they pick up lots of pollen to pass to the next flower.

Fragrant orchid

Epiphytes — plants that grow on other plants — are common in the rain forest. There are many different types — mosses, lichens, ferns, orchids, cacti, and bromeliads (members of the pineapple family).

Mosses and lichens

Alligator lizard

The rich plant life in the rain forest supports many species of insects, mammals, and birds. Bromeliads, which grow high up in the canopy on tall trees, catch rain in their circle of stout, prickly leaves. Poison-arrow frogs come to these pools with their newly hatched tadpoles (below). The mother frog comes back each day and lays an infertile egg for each of her tadpoles, to give them enough food to survive.

Dragonfly

Bromeliad

Skeleton butterfly

Poison-arrow frog

Poison-arrow frog tadpoles

Day-flying clearwing moth

The spider monkey uses its strong prehensile tail as a fifth limb to move quickly through the trees and twisted lianas of the rain forest.

Animal Paradise

The world's rain forests are home to 9 out of 10 non-human primates. 40 percent of all birds of prey live in them, and a staggering 80 percent of the world's insects creep around in the rain forests. As the rain forests are disappearing, many of these precious creatures are becoming endangered. Several species become extinct every day. The primates are one of the most vulnerable groups — some are on the verge of extinction with only a few hundred left alive. The woolly spider monkey, for example, is now extremely rare.

The emerald tree boa of South America (above right) blends in perfectly with its surroundings. It is a canopy hunter that prowls around at the tops of trees, coiling around branches and lying in wait for the small mammals, birds, and frogs that live there. It can grow up to 10 feet (3 meters) long.

The tree porcupine (far right) looks prickly, but it is considered a delicacy in West Africa. Hunting such "bushmeat" is putting great pressure on the survival of some species.

Spider monkey

Squirrel monkey

Emerald
tree boa

Red howler
monkey

Jaguar

Lianas

Tree
porcupine

11

Passion flower butterfly

Red-eyed
tree frog

Golden eyelash viper

Poison-
arrow frog

Iguana

Topaz hummingbird

Passion flower

Heliconid butterfly

Leaf-cutter ant

Hummingbirds drink nectar. Some rain forest plants put so many nutrients into their nectar that it is almost a complete food. Insects that drink the nectar can live on that alone. Larger animals, such as hummingbirds, supplement this diet with a few choice insects that they pick off the flowers they visit.

The topaz hummingbird (left) sips nectar from passion flowers. Each flower sprinkles pollen onto its head as it drinks. When the bird goes on to the next flower, the pollen is brushed onto the female part of the flower and so fertilizes it.

The vibrant colors of the red-eyed tree frog (center) are not just decoration. They warn other animals that the frogs carry potent poisons in their skin. Some native rain forest people use these frogs to load arrows with poison. They scrape the arrow on the frog's skin before going off to hunt.

Tree frogs have very thin skins, but they do not dry out high up in the trees because the air in the rain forest is humid and heavy with moisture.

Leaf-cutter ants (left) are an ingenious group of insects. They cut up leaves with their scissor-like mouthparts and then carry them back to their underground nest. The leaves are then chewed thoroughly, but not eaten. Instead, the ants "plant" them with spores from special fungi. The fungi grow, feed on the leaves, and then the ants feast on their crop.

Forest People

The Yanomami Indians from Brazil and Venezuela cover a large area each day in their search for food and wood for cooking.

The Yanomami diet is high in fresh fruit and plant material but it also includes fresh meat everyday — fish, monkeys, and wild pigs.

People have made the rain forest their home for thousands of years. The earliest record of this — from caves deep in the jungle in Borneo — dates back 39 centuries. However, finds like this are rare, and most rain forest people have left no trace of their existence. Everything they owned and used, even hardwood arrowheads that could once pierce the tough skin of a wild pig, has rotted away.

Today, 50 million tribal people live in the rain forests. Hunter-gatherers, like the Mbuti pygmies, are nomadic. They travel around constantly, setting up temporary shelters and hunting animals as they spot them. The Siriono of northern Bolivia also wander widely, but for part of the year they clear small plots of land to grow crops. Shifting cultivators, like the Iban Sarawak, depend more on the crops they grow, using the same piece of land for about three years before leaving it. Settled cultivators, like the Bantu in central Africa, stay permanently in one place and remove the forest cover from the area around them. They are the only type of rain forest dweller to keep herds of domesticated animals.

Shapono

The Yanomami are skilled hunters, using spears, longbows, and poison-tipped arrows.

Body painting is very important to the Yanomami. Red is the most common color but black is also used, to indicate bravery or mourning. Other decorations worn include macaw feathers used for headdresses and armbands. Children pierce their lower lips, noses, and ears with sharp sticks.

Members of individual Yanomami tribes live together in a large palm-thatched hut called a shapono (above). At the end of the day, all the Yanomami in the village come together for storytelling, joking, and gossiping.

*Orange-winged
Amazon parrot*

The Yanomami speak many different
dialects, but they all learn a "formal"
language that all members of each
different tribe can understand.

More than
20,000 Yanomami
live in the highland
rain forests around the
border between Brazil and
Venezuela. They are the
largest group in the
Amazon rain forest that
still follows a traditional
lifestyle. They combine
shifting cultivation with
hunting and gathering of
forest foods. The plantain,
a starchy type of banana,
is their staple crop.

The Yanomami's territory
covers 15,450 square
miles (40,000 square
kilometers). Until
recently, wars between
villages were common,
particularly in the center
of the territory.
Settlements were highly
fortified and groups
moved often to escape
enemies. Today, the
Yanomami's survival is
being threatened by road
building and mining, and
they are uniting to
demand protection
for their land.

15

From Floor...

The forest floor is a warm, gloomy place. The air is still, and everything drips with moisture. In the evergreen rain forests, very little light reaches the ground, and only a few shade-tolerant plants are able to grow. The first few feet are dominated by bare trunks and the buttress roots that support them. In more open forests, such as those on the edge of the rain forests that span Indonesia, Thailand, and India, there is a thick jungle of young trees, shrubs, and lianas.

Because the layer of soil in rain forests is thin, trees can only grow surface roots, which barely go underground. These cannot support a tall tree, so extra roots grow from the trunk, arching out to the ground all around the base of the trunk. The aerial roots in mangrove swamps perform the same supporting role, helping to keep the trees from being swept away by the pull of the water.

The forest floor is relatively quiet compared to the canopy, and sometimes it is possible to hear frog calls coming from underground. These could be leptodactylids, a type of frog that has left streams to live in small, damp burrows. Before the rainy season, a male calls to attract a female and, if successful, mates with her in the burrow. The female lays her eggs on his back, into a frothy substance that he has whipped up with water, air, and mucus. Inside this frog meringue, the eggs can stay moist until they are ready to hatch and swim out into the forest at the height of the rains.

Glass-wing butterfly

Coati

Oasis
hummingbird

Postman
butterfly

Tamadua
and its
young

Nine-banded armadillo

17

Blue morpho butterfly

Quetzal

Violet-eared hummingbird

Squirrel monkey   Three-toed sloth

18

Most of the flowers and fruits form in the canopy. These attract insects, animals, and birds, making this a place that is teeming with life.

...to Ceiling

One hundred feet (30 meters) above the forest floor, intense sunlight shines for many hours everyday onto the top of the canopy. Tall trees laden with epiphytes and climbers branch into a vast green umbrella. Most of the light is trapped by this dense layer of vegetation — less than 2 percent of it ever reaches the ground. The canopy is hot, with daytime temperatures averaging 90°F. Although the air is still damp, humidity among the highest branches rarely reaches above 60 percent.

The canopy is the powerhouse of the rain forest. The leaves here are the major site of photosynthesis. This is the process by which plants use energy from sunlight to change carbon dioxide and water into simple sugars. The food formed in this way nourishes the plant and also feeds all the animals that eat that plant.

If one of the trees in the canopy dies, light pierces the gloom of the lower levels. Seeds and seedlings react quickly and shoot up to be the first to fill the gap.

The three-toed sloth (center) is one of the slowest-moving animals on earth. It not only moves very slowly, appearing to be "frozen" for hours at a time, but it can also take up to a month to digest its food. Although it would make a good meal for jaguars and other predators, most do not notice the sloth as it hangs motionless and quiet in the trees, high up in the canopy.

Green-winged macaw

Harpy eagle

Glass-wing butterflies

By Day

In daylight, the canopy of the rain forest is brightly lit. The light dapples through the leaves and illuminates the magnificent colors of the birds, butterflies, frogs, and lizards. Some canopy dwellers use color to attract a mate, some to blend in with the exotic flowers and fruits. Others use it to warn potential predators that they are inedible or dangerous to eat. There are also the really clever ones that copy warning colors to pretend they carry a large dose of deadly poison.

Many of the primates of the rain forest are in danger of extinction. The woolly spider monkey, or miriqui (center), is the largest primate that lives in the rain forest of South America. Four hundred years ago there were 400,000 woolly spider monkeys — now there are only 11 groups, containing 400 individuals all together. The government of Brazil and conservation groups are trying hard to save it from extinction.

Some of the most spectacular birds in the world live in the South American rain forests. Keel-billed toucans (above right) have unremarkable bodies topped off with magnificent beaks. Surprisingly, the beak is not as heavy as it looks, since it is made of a light, hard material that is stretched over a web of bony struts. The beak still manages to scare off predators because it looks dangerous and is brightly colored to highlight its size.

Common iguana

Keel-billed toucan

Red-faced uakari

Saw-billed hermit hummingbird

Red-eyed tree frog

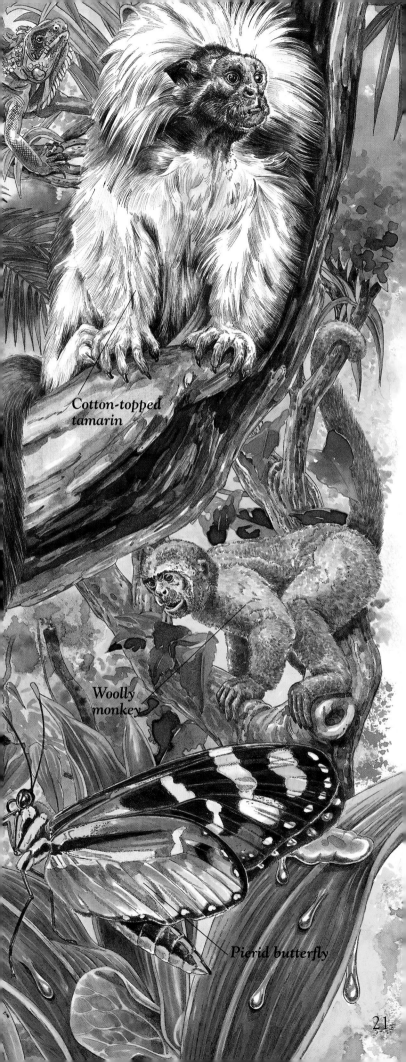

Cotton-topped
tamarin

Woolly
monkey

Pierid butterfly

21

Murine
possum

Three-toed
sloth

Olingo

Silky anteater

Owl
monkey

Hawk
moth

Pit
viper

Red-eyed
tree frog

By Night

At night, a totally different cast of characters fills the rain forest stage. Nocturnal animals, such as bats and sloths, and night-flying insects wake up. Moths and fruit bats tend to feed on the heavily scented flowers, as these are easier to detect in the dark. Many plants have become adapted for this and put their energy into creating scent instead of brightly colored petals. They rely on visits from nocturnal creatures for their pollination and also for spreading their seeds around the forests.

Olingos (center) are mammals from the same family as the raccoon and the panda. They are slender, 13-18 in (33–46 cm) long, with a very furry tail 15-20 in (38–51 cm) long. Olingos live in the rain forests of Central America and eat mainly fruit.

In order to reach its food, the silky anteater (center bottom) scratches a hole in an anthill with one of its sharp, curved claws. It darts its tongue in and out of the hole, capturing the ants and swallowing them whole. Though anteaters never attack another animal first, they will defend themselves fiercely. When in danger, they will fight off attackers with their thick, strong claws, which can be as long as 4 in (10 cm), making anteaters a match for even mountain lions or jaguars.

Red-eyed tree frogs (left) come from the rain forests of Costa Rica in South America. They have red eyes which serve as a defense against predators. If a frog is disturbed by a predator while asleep, the frog's eyes pop open. This sudden display of brightness startles the predator, as such large staring eyes could be those of an enemy, poised to attack. A moment's hesitation from the attacker is all the agile tree frog needs to leap to safety.

Undiscovered Treasures

Bromeliad

Tayra

The rain forest is not just an area of great beauty. It is also a cradle of life — a home to hundreds of people and a place where many rare species of plants and animals exist. Without this "store" of life, we do not know what might happen in the future. One area that is already losing out is medicine. Only a few plants have been tested, but many have already been found to contain substances to treat cancer or AIDS. How many more potential treatments have we lost already by clearing the forests?

The hoatzin (center) is one of the few leaf-eating forest birds of South America. The leaves can stay in the bird's stomach for two days while being digested by bacteria. This might explain why the bird smells like cow manure and flies very badly.

Hoatzin and its young

Death and Destruction

The world's ever increasing human population puts great pressure on the rain forests. By the year 2100, eight billion people will be living in countries that contain rain forests. In order to feed their people, these countries will need more farming land. That means more areas of rain forest will be cut down, cleared, or burned. More trees will be destroyed as fuel. The rivers running through the forests will be dammed to generate electricity and to allow roads to be built. Underground mines may be constructed to obtain the rich natural resources below. If such exploitation of the rain forests goes unchecked, they may never recover.

The rain forests are part of the earth's life-support systems. They affect weather patterns, and the trees hold the nutrient-rich soil together, preventing erosion. When acres of forest are cut down, flooding increases and large areas of soil are washed away. Once the soil is gone, no amount of human effort can re-establish the unique environment of plants and animals that made up the rain forest.

Hope for the Future

Rain forest that has been plundered can recover if it is left alone. New plants grow quickly to reclaim cleared land, and the thick new vegetation soon becomes filled with insects and small mammals. But leaving the rain forest alone is not really an option. Our need for its resources is too great. We have to think about how to use the forests in a sustainable way. That means taking what we want without destoying what it has to offer for future generations. We must remember that the rain forests are irreplaceable and invaluable to life on Earth.

We still need many of the products available from the rain forests — timber, latex, fruit, rattans, medicinal plants, rubber, oil, fibers, and cellulose. Latex is tapped from wild rubber trees by cutting slanting grooves in the trunk and letting the sap ooze out (above right). Plantations can provide these materials, without causing soil damage, if they are managed carefully.

Some parts of the rain forests must be kept untouched. Nature reserves have already been set up in rain forests all over the world (see right). There is one reserve for each type of rain forest ecosystem. These areas are protected but can still be studied to find out more about the value of the rain forests.

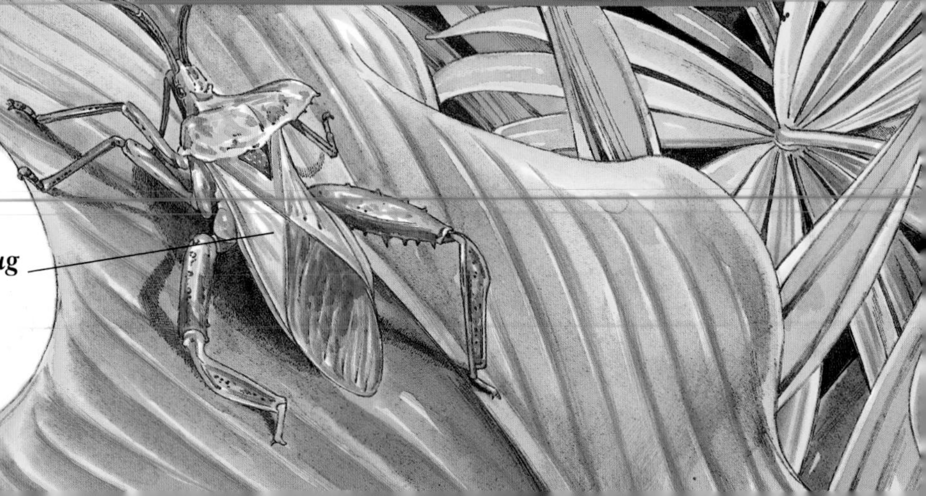

Stink bug

28

Oil wells (left) are an ugly sight in
the middle of a rain forest, but
they do surprisingly little damage.
Only small areas have to be cleared for
them and then most of their activities go
on below ground. Oil is also a very good
source of income. Some of the money it
makes can be used to fund conservation
projects.

Many wildlife conservation projects
are succeeding. In 1972, India set up
14 tiger reserves as part of Project Tiger.
At that stage, fewer than 2,000 tigers were
left in the country. Today, 9540 square miles
(24,700 square kilometers) has been put aside as a
protected habitat for the tigers. Their number has
stopped falling and is just starting to rise again.

The right of native people to live as they have lived for
generations is now being recognized. In some projects,
field workers from large companies are working with the
shaman (medicine man or woman) in different tribes to
identify rain forest plants that are used in traditional
medicines. If these are developed as modern medicines,
some of the profit made is given back to the tribe, whose
members use it to protect their tribal lands.

A shaman of the Kampa tribe (below left)
is preparing ayahuasca, a hallucinogenic
substance made from the bark and leaves of
certain trees. In the West, its ingredients
have been used to treat malaria.

White-tailed deer

Katydid

29

Glossary

Aerial root
Roots that stick out from the trunk of a tree, above ground level. Aerial roots have two functions: to prevent the roots from becoming rotten by being in water all the time; and as supports for a tall tree.

Altitude
The height of ground above sea level. The top of mountains are at high altitudes. Coastal areas are at low altitudes.

Canopy
The uppermost layer of the rain forest.

Conservation
The protection and maintenance of an environment, sometimes aimed at one particular species of animal or plant.

Deforestation
The clearing of areas of trees or forests.

Ecosystem
A living system that includes animals and plants.

Epiphytes
Plants that use other plants for support. Their roots never reach the ground.

Equator
The imaginary line around the center of the earth that indicates the parts of the planet that are always closest to the sun.

Evergreen
Evergreen trees and plants are those that never lose their leaves. They remain green and in full growth, year-round.

Extinct
A plant, animal, or any other living thing that has died out.

Habitat
The natural home of a living thing.

Hallucinogenic substance
Something that produces vivid waking dreams and a trance-like state.

Humidity
A measure of how much moisture there is in the air. High humidity makes people feel hot, clammy, and sweaty.

Liana
A type of climbing plant that grows in tropical forests.

Nocturnal
A creature that is active during the night and sleeps during the day.

Nomadic
Nomadic people move constantly from one region to another, usually taking their domestic animals with them. They rarely settle in one place for long.

Photosynthesis
A chemical reaction that plants use to feed themselves. They combine carbon dioxide from the air with water from the soil to make energy-rich sugars such as glucose. The energy to power the process comes from sunlight, and plants release oxygen as a by-product.

Poison
A substance that can cause injury or even death if eaten or taken in by a living thing.

Pollination
The sprinkling of pollen onto a particular part (the stigma) of a flower.

Predator
A type of animal that preys on other animals for food. Jaguars and emerald tree boas are both predators.

Prehensile
This means "like a limb." Many monkeys in the rain forest have

a prehensile tail that winds around branches, supports their weight, and serves as another limb.

Primates
The name for a subdivision of the animal kingdom that includes animals such as apes, monkeys, and people.

Rattan
A species of climbing palm.

Settled cultivators
People who settle permanently and set up farms.

Shifting cultivators
People who stay in one place for a while to grow crops and then move on to a new site after two or three years.

Soil erosion
The wearing away of the soil. Soil erosion is common in rain forest areas where the trees have been cut down. With no roots and vegetation to hold the soil together, it is easily blown or washed away by wind or rain. In this way the area loses its nutrient-rich soil and the land becomes dead.

Sustainable
Using a resource in a sustainable way means using it without using it all up. Planting fast-growing trees to replace those cut down for timber is a sustainable way of using forests. Cutting down old, slow-growing wild trees is not.

Swamp
An area of waterlogged ground.

Vegetation
All types of plants and plant life.

Rain Forest Facts

Most tropical rain forests have an annual rainfall of at least 100 inches (250 centimeters) and are filled with tall broad-leaved evergreen trees that form a continuous canopy.

Over $11,000 million worth of rain forest products, including rattan, bamboo, nuts, and spices, are sold every year around the world.

Deforestation (the destruction of trees) accounts for the loss of nearly two-thirds of Central America's rain forests — almost one million acres every year.

The most species-rich plot of rain forest known is in Peru: 283 species of trees were found in just 2.5 acres (1 hectare). Every second tree is a different species. While this particular area is the most species-rich, this kind of growth and diversity is typical of most rain forests.

In Sarawak, Borneo, the Penan people use more than 50 medicinal plants harvested from the forest. The plants are used for poison antidotes, contraceptives, clotting agents, general tonics, stimulants, disinfectants, remedies for headaches, fever, cuts and bruises, boils, snakebites, toothache, diarrhea, skin infections and rashes, and for setting bones.

Popular woods such as mahogany and rosewood, used for the manufacture of furniture, are found only in the rain forests.

Most of the nutrients in a rain forest ecosystem are stored in its vegetation rather than in its soil.

One of the biggest industries throughout Central America is cattle ranching. Most of the beef produced is exported to North

America for use in fast-food restaurants. The most common way to clear land for ranches is to tear down and set fire to the trees, a practice known as slash-and-burn agriculture. On September 9, 1987, a satellite picture of the Amazon River Basin showed a total of 7,603 fires burning in the rain forest.

The rate of rain forest destruction is such that species of plants and animals are becoming extinct and disappearing from the rain forests before they can be studied.

About 2,000 trees per minute are cut down in the rain forests around the world. In most of the countries with tropical rain forests, only one tree is replanted for every 10 cut down. In some countries the rate is one tree replanted for every 30 destroyed.

The largest threat to the survival of jaguars is the loss of the rain forests they live in. Their numbers have fallen fast, and they have already disappeared completely from many of their former regions. The only places they are still relatively common are remote areas of Guatemala and Belize in Central America.

Since the turn of the century, 90 tribes of native people have been wiped out in the Brazilian forests.

Twenty-six of those tribes were killed or dispersed in the past decade alone.

In the Himalayas, in Nepal, about a quarter of a million tons of topsoil are eroded away every year. This is due directly to the removal of the forests from that region. Even more soil is lost from the Himalayan foothills in India.

Western medical uses for plants discovered in rain forests include a medicine for malaria (the bark of the cinchona tree produces quinine); a muscle relaxant used during surgery (curare, a vine extract used by native peoples to poison arrows and darts); and a treatment for depression (secretions of a particular Amazonian frog).

Due to its specialized soil, rain forests are unsuitable for growing crops such as wheat and vegetables. Only trees and specialized vegetation thrive in such areas.

No one knows just how much the rest of the global ecosystem depends on rain forests, but we may find out in the next 30 to 50 years. That is how long it is estimated that it will take for tropical forests to disappear entirely, if current trends continue.

In the rain forests, there are some truly extraordinary plants. There is a fruit with more vitamin C than an orange, a palm with more vitamin A than spinach, and another palm whose seeds contain 27% protein. One type of tree produces a resin that can be used unprocessed to run a diesel engine, while another yields up to 660 pounds (300 kilograms) of oil-rich seeds a year.

31

Index